Sharks Don't Eat Peanut Butter...

Written by: Mark Privateer
Illustrated by: Jennifer Dunlap

To: The Kolacki Kids, Sharks rule! :-) Mark Privateer

M000237728

Amelia

Press
Buffalo, NY

Copyright © 2013 by Mark Privateer and Jennifer Dunlap

All rights reserved. No part of this publication may be reproduced, stored in a retrieval system, or transmitted in any form or by any means, electronic, mechanical, photocopying, recording, or otherwise, without the written prior permission of the author.

Printed in the United States of America

Privateer, Mark
Dunlap, Jennifer

Sharks Don't Eat Peanut Butter/ Privateer/Dunlap- 1st Edition

ISBN: 978-0989622066

1. Children's Book – Picture Book – Education. 2. Marine Life – Teaching – Amelia Press
1. Title

Amelia Press is an imprint of No Frills Buffalo

No Frills Buffalo Press
119 Dorchester Road
Buffalo, New York 14213

For More Information Visit Nofrillsbuffalo.com

From the Author

To my wife Kathleen and our three whirlwinds: Bryce, Mac, and Aspyn

From the Illustrator

To my three loves: William, Josef, and Jason

Alligators don't run marathons...

...but they have the ability to run short bursts on land at speeds that can exceed 30 mph.

Fast Fact: The longest recorded length for an alligator is 19 ft 2 in (5.8m).

B

eavers don't go to the dentist...

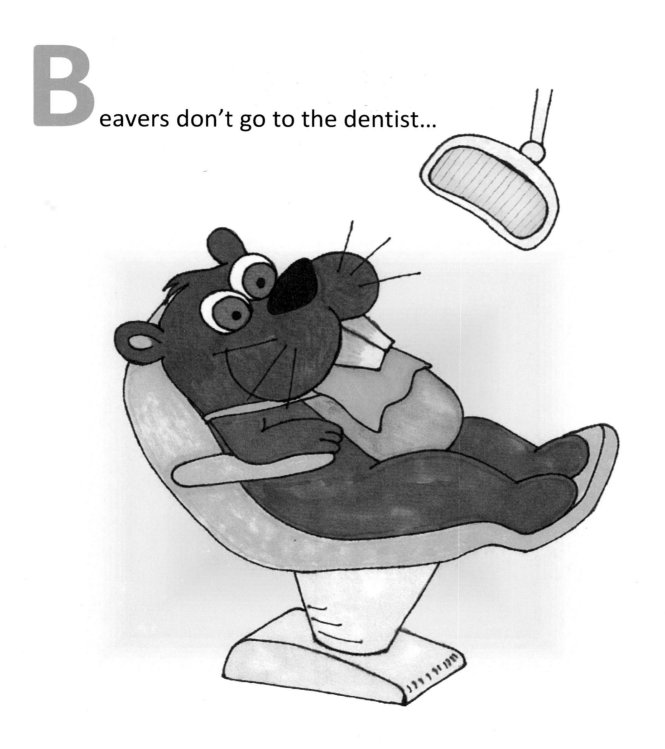

...but amazingly, their two front teeth never stop growing. Chewing on trees helps to keep their teeth from getting too long.

Vocabulary: The tough *enamel*, the hard substance found on teeth, on beaver's teeth gives them their orange to chestnut brown color.

Crawfish don't tap dance...

...but they do gracefully propel themselves backwards through the water when swimming. This is a faster and more efficient way for them to swim.

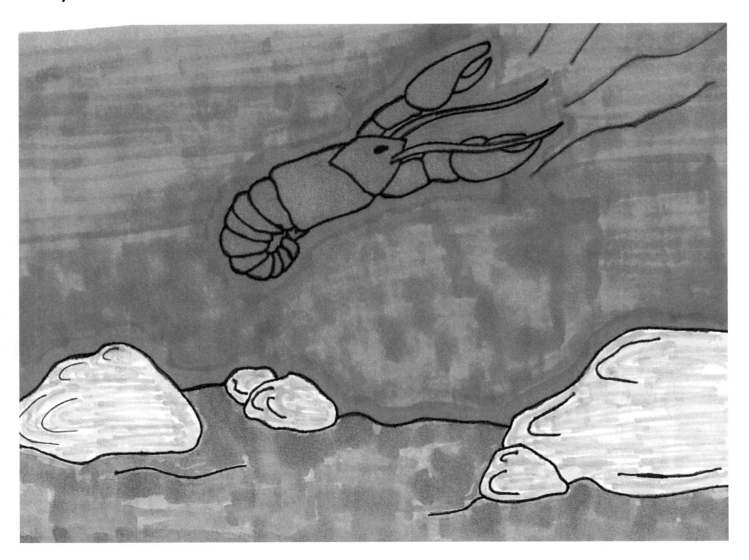

Fast Fact: There are over 500 different species of crawfish.

D olphins don't play basketball...

...but they can leap up to 20 ft out of water. Spinner dolphins get their name from the way they spin and twirl when they jump. Dusky dolphins jump backwards with their bellies to the sky.

Fast Fact: Dolphins have excellent eyesight, both in and out of water.

E els don't perform magic tricks...

...but they do tie themselves into knots. This helps them to catch and hold their prey.

Vocabulary: Eels lack **appendages**, a part or organ, such as an arm, leg, or fin, but they can quickly twist and turn their bodies to hold on tight to their prey.

F

rogs don't drive tanks…

...but a group of frogs is called an army.

Fast Fact: Frogs don't drink water; they absorb it through their skin.

Giant squids don't wear glasses...

...but they do have the largest eyes of any known animal, land or sea. Some giant squids have eyes as big as beach balls.

Fast Fact: Giant squids are very mysterious. The first images of a live giant squid in its natural habitat were not taken until September of 2004.

H

ippopotamuses don't scuba dive...

...but an adult hippopotamus can hold its breath and stay underwater for up to 6 minutes.

Vocabulary: When a hippopotamus is **submerged**, *to put or sink below the surface*, its ears and nose automatically close to keep the water out.

Ichthyosaurses don't wear Halloween costumes...

...but they are often misidentified as fish. Ichthyosaurses are actually reptiles, not fish.

Fast Fact: The name Ichthyosaurses translates to "Fish-Lizard".

J

ellyfish don't use walkers...

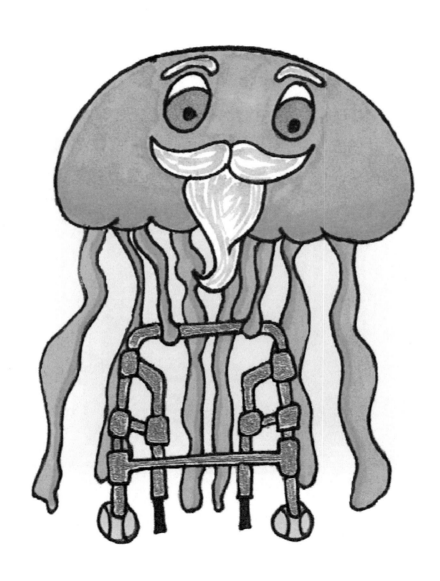

...but they have been around for more than 650 million years. Jellyfish are older than both sharks and dinosaurs.

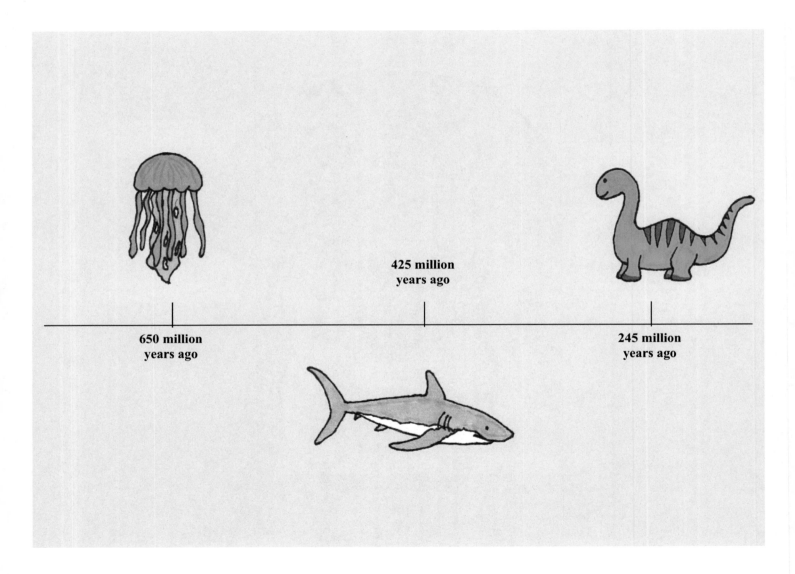

425 million
years ago

650 million
years ago

245 million
years ago

Fast Fact: Even a lifeless jellyfish can sting you.

K

iller whales don't listen to music...

...but they do hunt and travel in groups called pods.

Fast Fact: Male killer whales have the tallest dorsal fin of any whale; they can stand 6 ft (1.8m) high.

Lobsters don't lift weights...

...but a lobster's crusher claw can squeeze between 500-1,000 lbs per square inch.

Fast Fact: Lobsters can live to be 100 years old or older.

M anatees don't live on farms...

...but they are commonly referred to as the sea cow or "the cow of the sea".

Vocabulary: Manatees have paddle-like flippers with a fingernail on the end of them. This is a **remnant**, *something left over*, that evolved from when they use to live on land.

N arwhals don't compete in fencing...

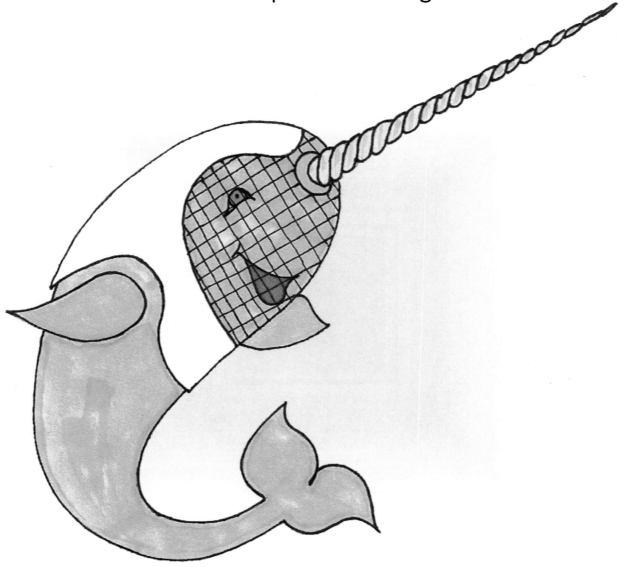

...but they do have a sword-like spiral tooth that can grow up to 10 ft long.

Fast Fact: The narwhal is very elusive and is considered one of the rarest whales in the world.

O

ctopuses don't perform circus tricks...

...but they can squeeze their bodies through a hole the size of a quarter.

Fast Fact: **An octopus has three hearts.**

Penguins don't text their friends...

...but they do communicate by using body movements called displays. These displays are used to communicate nesting territories, mating information and to help warn of intruders.

Fast Fact: Penguins sleep standing up.

Queensland groupers don't chew bubblegum...

...but they do have seven rows of teeth in the middle of their lower jaw.

Fast Fact: The queensland grouper can open and close its mouth so quickly that the human eye cannot even detect the movement.

River otters don't play on playgrounds...

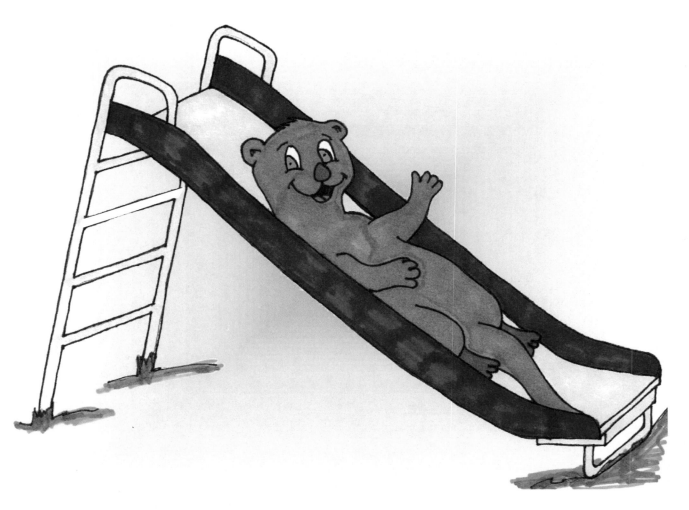

...but while playing and traveling on land, river otters have been known to slide up to 20 ft on their bellies.

Vocabulary: River otters live in all types of **habitats**, *a place where an animal normally lives*, as long as there is accessibility to high quality water and an abundant food supply.

Sharks don't eat peanut butter...

...but the great white shark can eat upwards of 500 lbs of food a day. After a large meal, a great white shark can live for more than a month without eating.

Fast Fact: Great white sharks swallow their bites whole. It can swallow an object half its size.

Turtles don't go on vacations...

...but leatherback sea turtles have been known to travel up to 3,000 miles between feeding and nesting grounds.

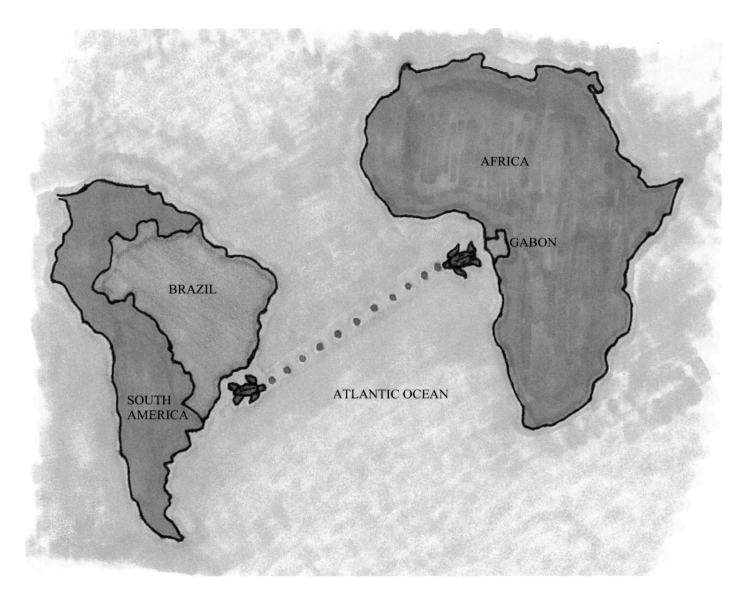

Fast Fact: One leatherback sea turtle was tracked traveling over 12,000 miles.

U

rchins don't have twin brothers...

...but they can split themselves to make an identical copy.

Vocabulary: Sea urchins' spines are solid in some species and filled with poison in others. They are used for **locomotion**, *moving from place to place*, and protection.

Velvet crabs don't play in bluegrass bands...

...but they are known as the fiddler crab because of the way their back legs move while swimming. Their legs move back and forth, similar to the movements a fiddler makes.

Fast Fact: Because of their red eyes and aggressive nature, the velvet crab is also nicknamed the "devil" or "witch" crab.

Walruses don't go mountain climbing...

...but they do use their tusks to dig into the ice. This helps them to climb out of the water and to move more quickly on land.

Fast Fact: A male walrus can weigh as much as 3,700 lbs (1,700 kg) and a female walrus can weigh up to 2,700 lbs (1,200kg).

X-ray fish don't wear armor...

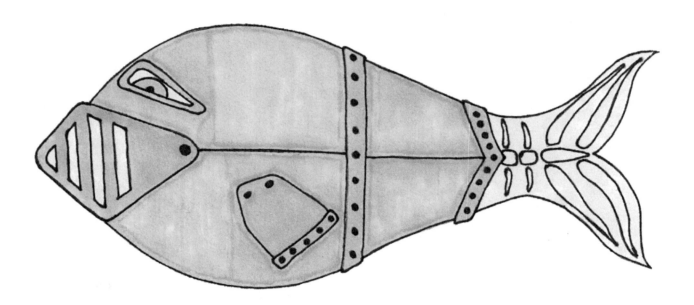

...but they do have transparent skin that helps them to blend into their surroundings. This helps protect them from predators by making them more difficult to see.

Fast Fact: Female x-ray fish are usually larger than the males.

Yellowtail clownfish don't wear bandages...

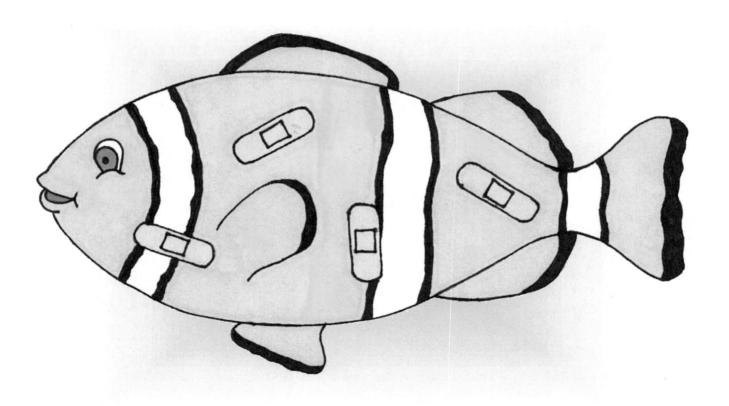

...but they do secrete a slime that protects their skin against parasites and infections.

Fast Fact: Clownfish and damselfish are the only species that can avoid being stung by an anemone.

Zebra lionfish don't know karate...

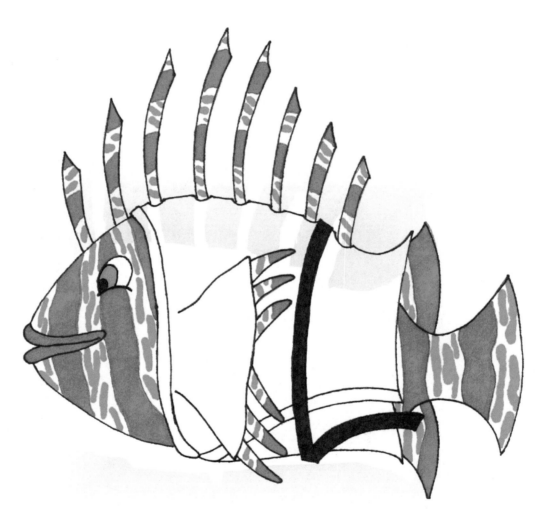

...but they do protect themselves with poisonous spikes on their backs. Lionfish are among the most poisonous fish in the world.

Vocabulary: Zebra lionfish are starting to **invade**, *spread over*, the Atlantic Ocean and are thriving in coral reefs along the Gulf Stream.

About the Illustrator

Jennifer Noble-Dunlap is a High School Technology Education Teacher. She currently resides in Western New York with her husband William and their two boys; Josef and Jason. Jennifer is an emerging artist who has shown her artwork at the Allentown Art Festival in Buffalo, NY as well as other local art shows.

About the Author

Mark Privateer is a high school teacher who has been teaching for over 12 years. He currently resides in Lake View, NY with his wife Kathleen and their three children; Bryce, Mac and Aspyn. This is his second published children's book. Mark is the author of the children's book *How to Tame a Macker*.